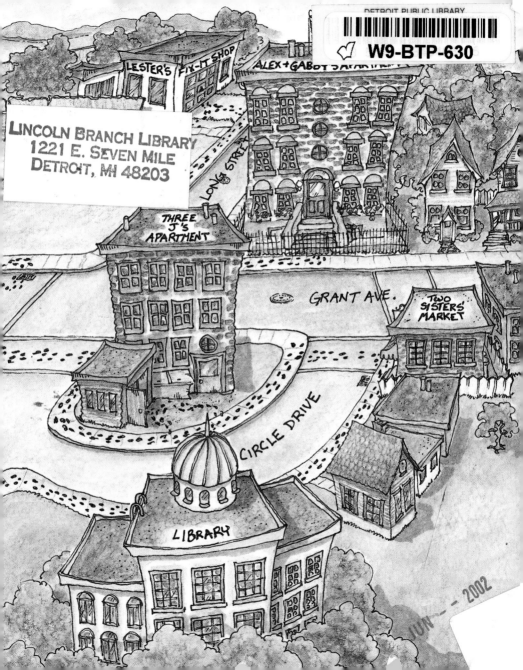

THE BIG, BEAUTIFUL, BROWN BOX

THE CORNER KIDS

Written by Larry Dane Brimner • Illustrated by Christine Tripp

Children's Press®
A Division of Scholastic Inc.
New York • Toronto • London • Auckland • Sydney
Mexico City • New Delhi • Hong Kong
Danbury, Connecticut

To Rosalie Heacock, for believing
—L.D.B.

For my son Eric
—C.T.

Reading Consultants
Linda Cornwell
Coordinator of School Quality and Professional Improvement
(Indiana State Teachers Association)

Katharine A. Kane
Education Consultant
(Retired, San Diego County Office of Education and San Diego State University)

Library of Congress Cataloging-in-Publication Data

Brimner, Larry Dane.
    The big, beautiful, brown box / by Larry Dane Brimner ; illustrated by Christine Tripp.
        p. cm. — (Rookie choices)
    Summary: The Corner Kids all have different ideas about how to use a big box, but
then they find that working together is the best idea of all.
    ISBN 0-516-22160-4 (lib. bdg.)   0-516-25973-3 (pbk.)
    [1. Boxes—Fiction. 2. Cooperativeness—Fiction.] I. Tripp, Christine, ill. II. Title.
III. Series.
PZ7.B767 Bi 2001
[E]—dc21   00-047564

This book is about

communication.

Three J looked out his
bedroom window.
Across the street in
the empty lot was a
big, beautiful, brown box.

"Wow!" he said.
"That will make a perfect fort."
He raced down the hall.

"Jeffrey James Judson!"
his father called.

Three J stopped.
He peeked around the corner.

"No running until your feet
hit the street," his father said.
"It's the house rule,
or did you forget?"

"Sorry," said Three J.
He walked to the front
door as fast as he could.

By the time Three J reached
the empty lot, Gabby and Alex
were there, too. They called
themselves the Corner Kids.

"This will make a perfect fort," Three J said. He grabbed one side of the box.

"It's going to be a race car," said Gabby. She grabbed another side of the box.

"No," said Alex. "It's going to be a pirate ship." He grabbed another side of the box and tugged.

Three J and Gabby tugged, too.

17

Before long, they were yelling and tugging, tugging and yelling.

All of a sudden, Three J heard a rip. "Stop!" he said as loud as he could. "We're tearing it!"

The yelling and tugging stopped.

"Let's try something," Three J said. "Let's think of two things we could make with this great box. You go first, Gabby."

"We could make a race car,"
Gabby said. "I guess it could also
be our clubhouse."

"We could make a pirate ship,"
Alex said, "but Gabby's right.
We've been wanting a clubhouse."

"That's what I thought," Three J said. "This box could make a great fort, but it would be an even better clubhouse."

Three J guarded the box while Gabby and Alex collected some supplies. Then they went to work.

27

They painted a sign.
They hung a door.
Alex's mother helped
them make a window.

That afternoon, the Corner Kids looked at their work. "It's the best clubhouse ever," they all said at once. Then they held their first meeting.

ABOUT THE AUTHOR

Larry Dane Brimner studied literature and writing at San Diego State University and taught school for twenty years. The author of more than seventy-five books for children, many of them Children's Press titles, he enjoys meeting young readers and writers when he isn't at his computer.

ABOUT THE ILLUSTRATOR

Christine Tripp lives in Ottawa, Canada, with her husband Don; four grown children—Elizabeth, Erin, Emily, and Eric; son-in-law Jason; grandsons Brandon and Kobe; four cats; and one very large, scruffy puppy named Jake.

SPINNINGWHEEL
BIKE
SHOP

COTTONWOOD SCHOOL

COTTONWOOD STREET

LONG STREET